EVERY SOUND IS NOT A WOLF

ALSO BY ALBERTO RÍOS

POETRY

Not Go Away Is My Name
A Small Story about the Sky
The Dangerous Shirt
The Theater of Night
The Smallest Muscle in the Human Body
Teodoro Luna's Two Kisses
The Warrington Poems
The Lime Orchard Woman
Five Indiscretions
Whispering to Fool the Wind
Sleeping on Fists
Elk Heads on the Wall

FICTION

A Good Map of All Things: A Picaresque Novel
The Curtain of Trees
Pig Cookies
The Iguana Killer

NONFICTION

Capirotada: A Nogales Memoir

EVERY SOUND IS NOT A WOLF

ALBERTO RÍOS

COPPER CANYON PRESS
PORT TOWNSEND, WASHINGTON

Printed in the United States of America

Cover art: Dave Newman, *Moon Over Surreal Desert.* Mixed media on board, 24 × 24 in. www.daveartnm.com

Copper Canyon Press is in residence at Fort Worden State Park in Port Townsend, Washington, under the auspices of Centrum. Centrum is a gathering place for artists and creative thinkers from around the world, students of all ages and backgrounds, and audiences seeking extraordinary cultural enrichment.

LIBRARY OF CONGRESS CATALOGING-IN-PUBLICATION DATA
Names: Ríos, Alberto, author.
Title: Every sound is not a wolf / Alberto Ríos.
Description: Port Townsend, Washington : Copper Canyon Press, 2025. |
Summary: "A collection of poems by Alberto Ríos" — Provided by publisher.
Identifiers: LCCN 2024043267 (print) | LCCN 2024043268 (ebook) |
ISBN 9781556597114 (paperback) | ISBN 9781619323124 (epub)
Subjects: LCGFT: Poetry.
Classificiation: LCC PS3568.I587 E94 2025 (print) |
LCC PS3568.I587 (ebook) | DDC 811/.54—dc23/eng/20240920
LC record available at https://lccn.loc.gov/2024043267
LC ebook record available at https://lccn.loc.gov/2024043268

9 8 7 6 5 4 3 2 FIRST PRINTING

COPPER CANYON PRESS
Post Office Box 271
Port Townsend, Washington 98368
www.coppercanyonpress.org

Acknowledgments

Academy of American Poets: “Taking Our Olympic Measure”

Cholla Needles: “A Dictionary of the Wind,” “Heading North Through the Sonoran Desert,” “Invisible Cord in the Invisible Outlet,” “I See the Bird and Am the Bird,” “The Mathematics of Oneself,” “The Shortest Song,” “The Twitch of My Eyebrow,” “We Are the Mapmakers of Sudden Change,” “What’s Happening”

Connotation Press: “Quietude”

Finger Exercises for Poets: “Pérez the Mouse”

James Dickey Review: “The Dance of Her Hand,” “This Voice That Spring Gives to the Orange Trees”

Lake Effect: “I’m Sorry but I’m Still Evicting the Pigeons”

The MacGuffin: “In Service to Service”

New Letters: “Noé, Who Spoke Best When He Did Not Speak”

Platte Valley Review: “The Migration of the Birds Away from Us”

Requited: “We Still Talk About You”

Studio: “As if It Were Him”

Superstition Review: “The Sheet Music of Place”

Talking River: “Build the Word True”

Thanks to Arizona State University and Copper Canyon Press for their abiding support of my work.

For Norman Dubie

Al agonizar el viejo marino pidió que le acercasen un espejo para ver el mar por última vez.

As he was dying, the old sailor asked for a mirror, that he might look at the sea for the last time.

Ramón Gómez de la Serna

CONTENTS

ONE

Enough to make good of it all

TWO

The small sirens and screams

THREE

I became two

FOUR

We have the power to be rain in the desert

FIVE

Theirs is a short life of light and crawl

SIX

The world, the world

EVERY SOUND IS NOT A WOLF

ONE

Enough to make good of it all

The Twitch of My Eyebrow

I went to Wanamaker's to hear the organ,
To the Embarcadero to taste some chocolate.

I've seen the tragic field of empty chairs, including the small ones,
Watched an osprey come down from the sky for a fish on the Snake.

I've stood on the inside of the White Dove of the Desert
And outside the cold city park made with antlers hung everywhere.

The eastern shore of the great lake frozen over seemed otherworldly,
As did the butterflies in their migration suddenly all over the windshield—

As I myself migrated home from a conference.
I have looked through the gray diamonds of the barbed-wire fence.

I've seen the rising wisps of steam meeting the falling flakes of snow
Create a gentle battlefront at the cold top of the world.

We have each done all of this. If not these places and these things,
Then others equally moving and permanently resident in our memory.

We have been places. We have moved around. We make room in ourselves
To remember. We taste other foods and store those tastes in our fondness.

I am all the people I have been who have done all of this.
I am crowded inside but have so far found enough space

To keep everyone seated, even as more are constantly entering.
When I smell something, one of them is sure to raise a hand

So quietly in recognition, that hand looking like an errant hair
Reaching out of an otherwise well-behaved eyebrow.

For Six Minutes, My Mother

For my mother, 1929–2016. Rara avis.

On my walk I fall in behind an older woman.
She is a stranger, or at least she seems to be.

I am still at a small distance and can't tell who she is.
The distance makes the lady herself smaller,

But the late afternoon angle of the sun makes her shadow large.
She walks slowly. The path is narrow.

I don't try to pass her so as not to rush her.
In this lady's movements, I see my mother—

In her clothing, in the shape of her, in her walk.
I do not try to pass her even when I can.

If I pass her, I know I will look at her face.
The face will not be my mother's.

My mother has been gone for a long time now
But she has left a trail of crumbs of herself

So that I will not be lost, even without her.
So that the trail will be clear.

This is not the her that is a picture, not the her in a frame on an altar—
The way people see her now.

But this is how she walked, over no ground in particular,
How she walked to get from here to there.

The real her. Not posed, not big-smiling, not perfectly combed.
This was her on a Thursday afternoon. A Monday morning.

I have seen this woman walking in front of me
Many times before, though it is always a different woman,

Each woman always my mother,
Showing me that my mother is all right.

I have learned not to shout out to her, knowing
I will only see a stranger's face and get a curious look.

It is never her and always her.
This is the time I get to spend with her now.

Over There

The neighbors on two sides of us have dogs. Occasionally,
Other dogs wander into the neighborhood on their own,

Happy in their loping moment but clearly nervous,
Eyes looking furtively all around—ears looking, too.

Thankfully, someone comes running for them every time.
Freedom has been good but being found seems joyous.

These dogs had not barked at all, not so sure about things,
And especially not wanting the wrong person to save them.

The dogs in the distance, however, the invisible dogs
Far away, they make a sound of their own, have a presence

In a place we cannot see. It's simply a general direction,
A home somewhere over there. So many dogs

Live over there. Perhaps it's where the dogs we have known
All go. Every so often, we can hear their distinct bark,

Though it's always attributed to some other dog.
We know better. Something in us hears what is ours.

Over there, wherever that is, has followed me around
All my life. No matter where I am, it is always around me.

It, and all the things I cannot see or hear clearly
But that I know, understand, remember, and hope to have near.

The dogs that wander into this neighborhood have wandered
Into their over there, and it is us.

I'm counting on us over there to take care of things.
I'm counting on us to make that place be what we imagine it to be.

The Artifact of Is

The desert is not always sun, not
Always cactus needles, not coyotes.

Sometimes, it is blue sky and spring day.
Most times, it is a place like any place.

It is simply where you are standing.
The desert is what you are feeling.

The desert has room for all the stars that you see
Then feel, all those sparkling specks

Familiar enough, looking maybe a little dusty
As if the dust that you see in the daytime

Goes up into the sky to work a night shift.
The world is at work, in everything and all the time.

When you walk in the desert,
You are always looking for something.

The desert is the size of your hunger, your curiosity,
The size of an absence you cannot fill.

Most times, it is not simply or only the desert.
It is the world so clearly alive with itself everywhere.

You pick up a simple quartz rock.
You hold in your hand the artifact of is.

Quietude

I have listened for what makes no sound,
Trying not to mistake it for silence.

This quiet is louder than anything
I have heard noise make.

Listen, if you can.
Nothing makes no sound.

It is long in its making where noise is fast.
It is slow in its unmistakable intensity.

I have worked all my life to hear it
As one might listen in the dark for a wolf.

Every sound is not a wolf—but one.
Every sound is not a breath stopped—but one.

I have listened, hoping not to hear
What wants not to be heard.

Those Years When She Was Acting as if She Were Not Falling

She pretended it wasn't happening, of course. Every time,
It was as if it had all been someone else.

Old woman. Grandmother. Wife so long ago.
All my mother could do now was fall,

To slip at every turn, her illness shoving her
As though it were standing at her back.

The bruises—so many—they bloomed
Into the bouquet of her, pansies and daffodils,

A magical rouge not applied but just suddenly there,
A theatrical staging of the skin not, perhaps, to look better

But to show that she was still a speaking-part actor onstage.
The bruise-flowers wilted but were then replaced

Often. These were not the flowers of a first dance.
She fell, she kept falling, until falling was all there was.

She explained each one away, persuasively, and with a laugh,
Even in the emergency rooms and through the hundred stitches.

Finally, she had to lie down to keep from falling—
This one exquisite gesture coming at the end of the final act.

Bedroom

Ceiling fan, gentle great-grandchild of the palm frond.
Book, you are a little second apartment inside this room.

Mirror, I would recognize you anywhere.
Bed, you are the space capsule we lie in as we prepare for liftoff.

Desk lamp, you make magicians of us all for half a second.
Curtain, you are ready to be drawn on the theater of the world.

Clock, you are the taxi meter tracking the ride of our lives.
Pillow, you are the patient childhood dog we still lie against.

Chest of drawers, you are the file cabinet of good looks.
Chair, secret love, we always come back, falling into your waiting arms.

Bedsheet, your wrinkles become our wrinkles.
Painting, you allow us to look through the wall at another world.

Carpet, you are the surprising mulch of a pine forest in the desert.
Blanket, under you I feel my mother's first, most profound hope for me.

As if It Were Him

El peso me quiere, she says to me,
Her grandson. *Weight loves me.*

We laugh but she says, *No,*
It is completely true. A willful creature,

Her husband. After Margarito's death,
She has let his hands come back to touch hers.

She has let him hold her. *It's taken all these years,*
But he has found a way to come back to me.

She has said *yes*, and *yes* again
As if that weight were him. *Yes*,

A shower of confetti and yeses
Spinning her to that kiss.

Weight loves me, she says,
Where no one else will. That man so long ago—

We are intimate again under my dresses.
He knows the folds of my skin.

Excuse me for saying so, she says—
Remembering for a moment

I am too young, but her happiness
Enough to make good of it all—

I am in love with this second man,
This husband new and all over me again.

Noé, Who Spoke Best When He Did Not Speak

His words were not stronger than his nod,
His eyes a better tongue than in his mouth—

He spoke by pointing with his chin,
By letting his eyes light on some object,

By indicating with his forefinger,
Sometimes two or three times to be loud.

Sometimes he spoke by not going somewhere.
Sometimes he went where he was not supposed to go,

In all cases wearing a look on his face
Nobody could misunderstand.

Sometimes his quietude was deafening. But
On those mornings when he ate what he liked,

The smile on his face said enough,
And meant everything to those who ate with him.

The Shortest Song

We know it's there. It waits to be heard.
It dares us to listen. We look at it and mostly try to resist.

The shatter of glass by itself is a jubilant sound,
A song rising as if from one of the curious instruments

Standing attentively at the back of the orchestra,
Called on infrequently but crucially, suddenly, to make

A sound like no other, a homage to the half-second moment.
The shatter of glass is wind through a chime,

Anger through a rock, intent through a fist.
The shatter of glass is the world made right

For someone, the world made wrong for someone else.
Immediately afterward, we are too busy—

Pick up the glass, sweep it up, report it, think about
Fixing it. We move so quickly forward that we do not

Whistle the song of the glass, or sing it to someone else.
It was a song so briefly, so sharply, it was sound-lightning.

It introduces itself so grandly but leaves just as quickly,
Nothing more than the flick of a lizard's tongue.

Its music is not played on the radio or in the car, a music
Surprising us with hello but that we remember as goodbye.

Goodbye something. Goodbye someone.
It is the song of *just once, just once* but unforgettable.

We Still Talk About You

Are you nervous? someone asks,
Looking at your jumpy leg.

It just happens, you say.
The ears on your head,

They are so small.
But your right leg itself has also listened,

Listened to something quiet and easy to miss
In the relaxed talk between friends.

Then it tells your hip what it has heard,
The whole right half of you now a little jumpy.

Of course, this half of you speaks
To your other side, which then moves as well.

This other side of you cannot help itself, either.
It's like a song has gotten stuck inside of you,

Or a secret, or some kind of happy news,
So that now both sides of you are jumpy.

You get up and begin to walk,
Trying to shake it off,

But then you run, then run faster,
Until you run fast enough

To talk to yourself young, all those years ago,
This is how you used to run!

You feel that young feeling again. You run until
Your feet are so fast they both leave the ground.

You find yourself in the wind,
Until suddenly you *are* the wind.

You are running so fast
You gain altitude, flying low.

Then the wings that are your arms
Make a break for it as well, spreading

Enough that they gather you, lift you,
And all of you goes.

Come back, come back! people shout,
The ones who saw it all,

Come back! they shout but they don't mean it.
They watch you go as their own legs,

Their own arms, their own bodies listen,
All of them wanting to go with you.

TWO

The small sirens and screams

The Increment That Builds the Night Sky

We assume the increment is upward:
I am a person,

I live in a neighborhood, in a town, somewhere
In a state, which is part of the country. We add up.

My country is on Earth, which is one planet
Among so many, followed by so many trillions more.

But the increment of adding up may be altogether wrong.
The freckle-lights in the sky,

They shine toward us, not away.
The lights are coming, all of them.

Earth is made of land and water masses,
Divided into many nations and seas,

Each country full of cities, of towns,
My town full of many inhabitants, then just me.

The increment, the increase, the star trail
Moves toward me. Toward you. Toward

Each of us, into the grasp of the small universe
We harbor inside. We feel it, we know, we cry.

We think these things come from something that happens
Outside us. But the crying, the joy, the intensity—they are

Something of their own. The increment is not away from us
But toward us, infinitely.

In describing this, I feel like an accordion of perspective,
Caught right in the middle—and I am,

And this is my music, which comes from somewhere
Inside me, even as I sing it out to you.

Things So Loud and Their Quietings

The world is loud but my life is not,
Quieted by its myriad attentions to, for example,

The operatic soprano door hinge.
The television news carries on,

As if it had not heard the diva hinge sing,
As if it had not heard my own news:

I finally softened the hinge's voice with a spray of oil—
Me! Powerful and capable as I am.

But curiously, I miss it,
The high note perhaps meant to be exactly what it was,

Warning me with this sound. It sings of something
But in a language that is not clear to me.

The high-pitched noise drowns out everything,
Then the quiet lets everything in, so that here we are.

Have I been warned sufficiently? The world, its squeaks,
Goose honks, bird chirps, and muffler-less cars,

Its quiet lightning bugs trying so hard to be loud:
Have I been warned sufficiently?

Something is happening. Still, the oil on the hinge
Has worked well.

For good or for bad, it has given me yet more time
Not to worry. I can fix a door hinge.

This Voice That Spring Gives to the Orange Trees

The week is March ending and almost April.
The orange tree in the side yard is full of white blossoms

Producing a redolence thick as scented wool in the air,
All of it pleasant, unbelievable to the nose, and happy.

I stand under the tree and listen to its hum, so many bees
At their work and with their full attention, their shoulders

Pressed hard against the white, waxy buds.
Their droning wings make the tree seem alive.

A full spring tree, blossomed in white, trembling
Bride of Frankenstein–like in its quiver of life.

But underneath it all, during job interviews and in their off-time
Gym talk and corner bar occasional meetups,

Bees want with their sound to be bigger, to be cicadas, practicing the hum
Bolstered by the steroids of a far-off, ubiquitous lawn mower.

But cicadas, too, with their incessant single-buzzing manner
Want to be electrical lines hit by lightning, or office door buzzers—

Office or warehouse door sounds, both of which are more serious
Than the pleasing and melodic, even beautifully orchestral

Doorbells of homes, which cannot be taken seriously, and which,
In these wild days, nobody answers anyway.

Those buzzers, then, in a brilliant strategy perfected by the Four Seasons,
Move to falsetto, the low sound becoming higher-pitched car alarms,

Upper-register sounds—the right side of the piano keyboard,
With occasional breaths, shouts really, Little Richard,

Screams when all is said and done wanting to be nerve endings,
Screams—more than heard—meaning so simply to be felt.

I See the Bird and Am the Bird

For my eye to see a bird,
My line of sight must reach it,

Extend from me to wing and, thereby,
In some fashion touch it:

However small the bird in my eye,
I am in flight, moving through its air, sparrow alive.

Something in my eye becomes an arm
Able to stretch out my hand to make contact,

To bring something back to me
Whole and intact. For that moment,

The bird and I are in each other's company,
The sky so suddenly inside us both.

Avenue of the Birds

Wind blew.
The trees stood regardless,

Shaking their thousand bony arms and shoulders,
Doing their little dance, every one of them,

As if they were teenagers, these trees,
Though they were well into their sixties.

The trees shook
And this would infuriate the wind, of course,

Who felt made fun of, who felt
The sighing of the trees was a jeer behind its back—

Something said not quite loud enough.
But the wind had no ears and did not know this was untrue.

The trees spoke but they said other things,
Busy helping the nesting birds and small creatures.

Trees and wind.
Theirs was a centuries-old misunderstanding.

One made the avenue of the birds
While the other made their home.

Theirs was no handshake, but they worked together
Even as they felt at odds with each other.

The trees liked to throw everything into the wind,
Letting it do the moving, the pruning, and the walking

They would have struggled with otherwise.
Trees took several-hundred-year vacations this way,

Throwing themselves as seed into the wild air
Only to be carried away by the wind,

Wind thinking it had won.
But enough patience saw those seeds go on to other places,

Germinate, become trees themselves,
Trees who then did the same all over again,

Until finally the trees came home to themselves.
The wind was too busy to notice their familiar faces.

So the trees danced all the more, happy,
While the wind kept at its angry, endless work.

I'm Sorry but I'm Still Evicting the Pigeons

The soft gurgling of the pigeons stirring
Is a nice sound in the morning,

Curious, like the purring of a cat but sized to the pigeon.
In that sense, it is loud: quiet on paper but loud in practice.

When they congregate outside my bedroom window,
The eaves make the sound even bigger, the pigeons

Seeming more rabbit-sized, the big kind of rabbit.
In their comfort my own sensibility is lulled too much,

Lurching at the mellifluous sounds. We can't live together
This way, not well, not for more than a few sunrises.

To keep the pigeons away I blast them with water.
I feel bad doing it. But I feel bad as well

Looking at the side of the house under the eaves
Where they have created a waterfall of their own living.

I rationalize that it's only water I'm shooting at them,
Their single-mindedness against my own,

All of us in a kind of game. Every hour, I spray water
Where they have found harbor.

I am the train going by their apartment at midnight,
The brash motorcycle so suddenly speeding up.

It is their house, I understand, but it is my house, too.
It is summer and the world is big—

I know they will find a new place to roost.
But the trouble of it all—I wouldn't want it myself.

A Dictionary of the Wind

We listen to the wind
Not as if it speaks words

But for what its words mean,
Its mile-long vocabulary of sighs,

Whispers clear in their meaning
From the centuries of their making:

We recognize wind on our skins—
We see it ruffle our hair, smell its scent,

But we do not listen to it
Except perhaps as a faraway fancy

Through the walls
Or as it holds up our arms for us

As we stand against it, playing.
But it is a bear too.

Round then as a drill in its tornado
Trying not to lash out, not wanting to hurt us.

But the wind has so many arms.
It tries but cannot always help itself

Or us, even as it tries to warn us.
However, its words are not ours,

Nothing captured in the catalogues of a dictionary.
Wind pronounces *dance* instead—

Pure movement, haunting sounds,
Hard motions, whispers and roars,

Hummingbirds and irritated mountain lions.
Its meaning does not come from a dictionary

Inside a library.
It is a world, a day, a feeling on the skin,

A downed mesquite, a pelican confused.
It calls upon a dictionary unpublished,

Not for sale but given freely
In the billion wild movements of its leaf pages.

Wind speaks in a late August full of storms,
A small draft in April. It speaks

With breath that everyone has breathed out,
All those old words made new.

We have not learned its language
Even as we expected it to learn ours—

But it has been here longer, and will outlive us.
We similarly assume

The future will speak our words.
But there is another language ahead.

Twenty Minutes in the Backyard

The house sparrow flies to the ground
To get the seed that has fallen from the feeder.

In doing so, it flies through a bit of spiderweb
Which works as something like a phone call

To the spider, who then answers with a *hello*,
Careful and very quiet, but nobody is there.

This happens a lot to spiders.
It makes them grumble about the neighbors

Who walk across the spider's curious lawn.
But the complaint is hollow—sometimes

Someone is indeed there, a fly, a moth,
Any number and manner of very small beast.

Each tries to run away but is tripped up
By the long, thin fingers of the web.

The small thing quivers, asks politely, *please*
To be let go, followed by a sincere apology.

But a spider does not have ears. This explains
Why it does not hear the house sparrow

Swoop up into the air, high enough
To reach the spider. Few leaves rustle,

While the whole world simply moves forward.
This is the Saturday business of the immense

Backyard conglomerate at work.
If one listens, one might hear

The great, bustling city of it all,
The small sirens and screams,

The caterpillars backing up,
The geckos at their mysterious work.

Vernal Equinox in the Desert

The Sonoran Desert—that word *sonoran,*
It means to be full of sound, sonorous,

Soundful, made from the music of a hundred noises
Played all at once in this place, the crickets

In their serenade to the rabbits at their work,
The stars so thick in the night that they hum.

To see this desert you must listen to it,
The shy, frightened rustle of a rabbit in the brush

Hushing her babies, the inching of beetles
So awkwardly left and right of straight—

Their small lumbering is dance.
Teenagering lizards speed in their fast

Hot-rod bodies over the simple song of all this,
Entering the big cities from the far fields.

Animal to animal, urban to rural, dark to day,
Them to us, and us to them:

In the desert, we dare one another to stay alive.
It is a watchful day, equinox, which makes the sound

Living likes most, half sun, half shade, half night,
Half day, all of it perched on a bridge of noon,

All the sounds in the world soothed
In this moment and in this place.

Today the sun will rise due east and set due west,
True as a compass, compass before compass,

Ancient. Today, on this day, things stand in balance,
And at this moment, we can be happy for one another.

THREE

I became two

We Are the Refugee

I have arrived from always
And I am going everywhere.

I am who you were, your parents,
Their parents. I come from the land that gave you

The shape of your hands. At night,
We all hear family stories of somewhere else.

The journey is simple enough: there
To here, even though nothing is harder.

The stories say, the desert cold at night
Then just as hot in the afternoon.

There is no middle ground, no rest.
From hot to cold, I stand between,

Straddling the miles of the journey, one foot
Hot, one foot cold, the rest of me unsure.

This journey of quiet tears has no end.
I live in the country of always walking.

Soon enough, I will be the mesquite and the cactus.
You will know me as the wind.

The family stories, they're true.
And they're all about you.

We Are the Mapmakers of Sudden Change

Change is the country no map tells you about.
Change is a secret destination to which you are invited

And cannot refuse, no matter the grand plans you have made.
You simply go, you must go, you will go.

On a small map, what happens next seems just a half step away,
A trifling step. But brought to scale, it is a massive leap in a life lived.

We want to go *over there:* but instead, we stumble over a rock.
We cut an onion too vigorously. Someone else drives too fast.

Then suddenness takes over. Suddenness, the like-it-or-not
Measure of change, which makes clear there is no going back.

You are going on a new adventure in this country with no name.
It may be fun.

Invention, innovation, the arts: these are one side of suddenness,
The human forging and making of the welcome new.

Tragedy, heartbreak, and loss, however, are its very real other side.
In the one, the words are *epiphany*, *connection*, *eureka*, *aha!*

While in the other, the words are all simply *oh no*—
All of them a vocabularium of the new moment's geography.

My mother as a young teenager lived through the Battle of Britain,
Her hometown being bombed every dark night.

She and her younger sister had the game of going outside each morning
To see how much new shrapnel had embedded in their front door.

We find our way through change, each of us. When we get lost,
The only way to find this place's map is to understand there is no map.

No directions are handed to us. We struggle with the language.
We have led the way through change, so that now the map is ours to make.

Forward is our magnetic north and is all we have—but it is a great deal.
Through the fairy-tale bramble of all suddenness and fear: *Onward.*

Pérez the Mouse

The Tooth Fairy or Pérez the Mouse—
When you lost a tooth on the border,

You had twice the chance that somebody would pay attention.
The Tooth Fairy had all the books and cartoons,

But El Ratón de los Dientes, the Tooth Mouse,
Came in whispers from grandmothers.

And the Tooth Mouse had a name, El Ratoncito Pérez,
A name that everyone knew but was quiet to say.

The border world so often worked in that manner—
What the books and television and school said,

That was one thing, a very big thing,
But what someone whispered, that was another.

At school, in English, and with friends, it was the Tooth Fairy.
But at home, with family, with Nana, it was different.

The happiness in this was that, no matter what happened,
There was always another way.

And besides, a fairy—no one had actually ever seen one.
But a mouse, this carried a different kind of weight.

The names of the mouse and the fairy came either with tears
And sopa de arroz, or laughter, a big gap, and morning anticipation,

The profound exchange of a tooth put under a pillow
For something else, something new, something exciting.

The exchange was meant to soothe, to be a salve, to quiet—
To say that giving a part of yourself meant something.

It is a story for children, of course,
And yet as adults we are the first to speak these names.

We want them to be remembered because we remember them.
In that moment we are saying, *We want what we do to matter.*

Invisible Cord in the Invisible Outlet

A circuit is an equation, is a sentence, is an epiphany,
Is a bridge between two shores,

Is the correct answer on the multiple-choice exam,
Is the black mark entered into the oval on the ballot,

Is the voyage between where you were then and now you are here,
Is whatever connects the ball thrown to the leaping dog,

The dog mouthing it out of the air, is the eye seeing a bird in flight
Then feeling something in the body not gravity.

The word *circuit* has many meanings but this is about electricity,
The world so charged with the current and voltage and power of itself.

Light, fire, movement, breathing, singing—these are the common lightning,
Hummingbirds everywhere, the glint after glint on the crests of the waves.

Fences and walls and dams and red Stop signs and *halt!* do not stop it,
Any of it. The short circuit is in constant repair.

Throw a ball to a child and watch it go sailing past the glove.
Watch someone come over, pick it up, and know to throw it again.

Raging Sea Monsters

The birds are fewer, the air warmer, the cars
Shove their fast way hard through it all.

Saying all this is easy. Of course we complain—
The newspaper is made of unhappy headlines

Somewhere in every edition.
But the birds used to be flocks—the flocks

Are fewer. The warmer air has become the warmest.
Cars are the reproducing rabbits of machines.

Again, it's easy to say all this, and we do, all the time.
But the bees are going somewhere without us.

The sun insists itself in the desert summer—
It cannot be any louder in saying *I am here.*

The wind irritates us until it is hard to ignore,
But we do. The water roils, thirsty for itself.

All this noise, all this noise, all these things.
Problems, headlines, news, conversations, sunburns—

It is all a bulletin tinnitus, an overload to the ear,
A crowding of the brain. Every day

We are called upon to be Hercules, to be Atlas,
To be Solomon in our world—

It turns out, however, that we are just our small selves.
We are readers of great stories, not authors of them.

Still, the call for watching out, for being careful—
It's there. It's there. We knew how to get this far

But the map, now, is old again, and like all old maps,
It draws raging sea monsters in the mysterious deep.

Perhaps the old maps were right.
Perhaps we did not conquer what we thought we had.

After So Much Border Talk, There Comes a Gray Time

Solvers of problems, speakers of languages,
Meeting-goers, tie wearers, handshakers:

As we stand at the border visiting, the sky is gray,
From nature, from cars, from weariness.

We are standing in a gray hour, dusk or dawn—
So tired but we cannot say. The hour is sudden to us,

Surprising, the way the setting or the rising of the sun
Always is—it has snuck up on us.

But what today offers us, unrelenting gray upon gray,
This is the surprise, gray's full suitcase flung open,

Preparing us to stay for what seems like
The longest stay an hour has ever made.

Time stands still in this color. Dusk or dawn,
Gray makes all hours interchangeable.

In this moment, time could be going forward
Or today could be yesterday. We cannot tell.

We try to solve problems but they are all the problems
That have ever been.

These are the talks.
These have always been the talks.

The Lake but More the River That Feeds It

The small river is not the placid place it appears:
Horseflies, air plankton, fish leaps, and reeds,

They are all there, quiet in their moment,
Leaving the geese to their echoing honks.

The water of this river moves straight, here,
Into the flow, the telling of time not circular at all,

Always forward, never back, always moving.
What the river brings is new water,

Nothing the same though nothing looks changed.
The river's show of water has moved on,

Taking its day with it, its traveling circus.
The ducks that came here yesterday are gone.

Today's ducks are all new, no matter how much
They resemble yesterday's quacking crowd.

A single day on the river has changed them
So much they do not lead the lives they led.

They are new birds. The ducks, the herons,
The storm-lost pelican blown over the mountains.

Today is a whole life, and will not be tomorrow's.
Every day is like that. Every day is a piano key,

The world and the water sounding a glissando
High to low, low to high, one boulder at a time.

In that current of timeless waters, so many are lost.
When the river reaches the lake

People bring bread and popcorn, cracked corn and grapes—
There are fish for the taking in the water—

But life on the river has left its lingering mark.
The ducks eat today but only today.

What tomorrow is, even on the lake,
Will be left to the animal they will be.

Small Secrets and Gray Books

When this dry world is cold,
Winter water blooms

A hundred small ways,
Sturdy pencils growing

Up from the ground, writing
Their story in a reedy script

Made of crossed branches.
There is more.

Mesquite books, barrel
Dictionaries, jacaranda

Promising purple love stories:
This place writes itself

In its branches and in the cracked
Caliche, in the cursive

If jagged Russian thistle, songs
Written in the note placement

Birds choose, sitting on a staff of wires
Strung everywhere.

To open the book of this place is to stop
Sitting still—

A change in everything comes next.
The heart's ship moves,

Traveling rough
But through

The harbor spaces
This November desert shows to us.

Heading North Through the Sonoran Desert

The fastest way to move is to move slowly,
To take our lesson from the moon, not the javelina.

The tortoise lives a hundred years but the roadrunner
Does not, no matter how it seems to arrive before it has left.

We are not those cartoons. We look to the animals for truth.
It is a Tuesday night somewhere. But traveling, moving

This way, here it is simply night, all the time. Only dream.
We close our eyes to the light, sleeping in the day.

When we open our eyes once more, it is to darkness again.
We seem to have stopped using our eyes, stopped needing them.

The gray night shadows, however, slowly start to show themselves,
The sounds around us keeping us careful, jackrabbits and owls.

We wear shoes but we wear the other shoes too,
The fragments of carpet cut a little bigger than our feet,

Carpet or worn tire tread or plastic bottles—anything not human,
A little more square, so that when we walk we won't make

Shoe tracks, people tracks. Nothing for someone else to see.
The walk is heavier this way but the distance is better, a better

Chance, no evidence along the winding rough sand in the arroyo.
The nameless bushes dried to thorns whip through our pants,

Making red the part of us that will be our rescue. We
Keep on, we look down, we fall forward, we fall forward again.

Thirst beyond all else—we try not to let water leave the body
But our legs drag, filled with mud made from tear-water and dust.

Still, our legs do their work even when we can't feel their muscle.
Our legs, which seem to call on the ancient animal inside them.

The Mathematics of Oneself

The slough of a rattlesnake, the wisping smoke
Rising from a finished-roaring campfire,

The let-off and left-over, the fuming and the loud—
Every border is a move from that to this,

Old skin to new, smooth from wrinkle, then to now, day
To night back to day, summer's merciless heat to autumn grace:

All this so that we come to understand that nothing stays
As is. Nothing sits still for very long. The world simply moves.

In this sense, no border is one border. Every border is so many:
A ready feast, a continuing festival, a traveling circus of imaginary

Delights, a border with its improbably perfect third-grade ruler line,
Making two half notes out of a whole, two halves of a family.

The very real imaginary line between countries, it pretends
To be a wall but is not overly effective, not to the senses—

The smells of herbs, the shades of colors painted onto houses,
The parsed difference between here and just over there.

The line is on the map but not in the place. On a map,
The color of a country is different, one from another,

But the colors of the street and the bougainvillea,
The colors of foods and shoes, none of it is finally different.

Still, the border is there.
Myself, as I stepped from one side of the border to the other,

I did not change, though I was changed.
I became two.

I became the odd mathematics of myself,
The one of me never able to be just one anymore.

FOUR

We have the power to be rain in the desert

The Dance of Her Hand

At the end of the sixties I was readying myself for graduation,
Nogales High School, but it was still weeks away.

For now, it was simply slow desert spring.
So much was happening in the world, so much except here,

Time moving not at all. But there were Friday dances.
They cost money and I had none and couldn't ask,

But I was in the Honor Society
So I got into school things free, which mattered.

It's hard to say this now but it mattered.
I could not have afforded to go otherwise.

That membership card allowed me entrance to a big part of my life.
I didn't have a car so I hitchhiked everywhere—

My family lived outside town and after school this was the way
To get back into town: hitch a ride, find a way, make a path.

It was like that with so many things. As with the Honor Society card,
Without hitchhiking, in the great rurals of the world,

There was nowhere else but the cowfields.
On this night, the darkness was warm and the live band was loud,

Their guitars and drums revving up like the start of a race.
I could hear it all from across the football field as I walked to the gym.

At the door, I showed my Honor Society card and got the nod,
Joining the crowd in the wooden embrace of the gym's auditorium.

Everyone did what they did every time at a dance—
First, they stood along the walls, talking to friends,

Pretending not to be particularly interested in dancing.
But then, as the first brave dancers took the floor,

Everyone's interest turned to looking at them. People laughed,
But it was not a mean laugh. Nobody knew how else to act.

Laughing was a way of saying *yes*.
And as the few dancers moved forward, the group along the wall

Started to close in around the dance floor
So that it became much more intimate, tribal.

This was perhaps the last high-school dance for many there,
Though nobody was thinking that.

We rarely saw the ends of things, only their beginnings.
Instead, we were thinking our high-school thoughts,

As always. It would take work to understand things better,
Work and time. Not everyone would make the journey forward.

I saw a friend of mine, Marcos, and we stood next to each other,
Which was far better than standing alone.

Nobody ever said that but nobody ever really stood alone either.
We talked for a bit and went over to get some punch.

Then I had an idea. I explained it to Marcos and he was in,
Even though he was shy. Even though I was shy.

Even though shy times two doesn't usually get anyone very far.
I said we have nothing to lose, which was mostly true.

I said what we should do is go around the dance floor person by person
And ask every girl, without exception, to dance. Every one.

We could have asked boys, too, but neither of us thought of that.
And before we could change our minds, we just asked. Every one.

The plan was slow at first, and we were nervous to start.
But after the first yes, we caught on with everyone. No skips.

It soon became evident what we were doing.
There was a sound underneath all the sound in the room,

A something that said we were coming, a laughing.
Nobody refused. It was roaring and it was work,

Dancing every dance.
Perhaps not everyone wanted to dance but everyone wanted to play.

Everyone wanted to be part of the story of this night.
Marcos and I stayed near each other, just to check in,

But the night took over and the game would not be unplayed,
This game that was not a game but simply a night different from others—

A feeling that is worth a lot in a small town.
The life-changing personal seriousness of a high-school dance—

This was, instead of that, fun. Just fun.
Everybody. The may-I-have-this-dance became a small conspiracy

The whole room shared, and gave itself up to.
About two-thirds of the way through the group,

She waited. She was clearly still unsure I would ask,
Which in retrospect makes me very sad. I had not skipped anyone

And I would not skip her.
She was much bigger than I was, heftier, and I could not recall

Anyone ever having asked her onto the floor
Though I had seen her at all the dances.

We were friends at a distance but she was one class younger,
And in the law book of high school this made connections harder.

But I did know her. I did.
She had a good smile and eyes that laughed and cried at the same time.

She used that smile on me and I returned it as best as I could with my own.
I reached out my hand to her, and it was like a deep breath being drawn—

By both of us. I was outside myself in that moment.
I held her hand. But in the holding, I could tell right away

Her skin did not feel like my skin.
Her skin had a layer of hand I did not have.

It was as if in holding her hand I were holding a glove.
It took me half a second and a whole life of retrospect

To realize that her life was not like my life.
Her hand I've come to understand came from a life of work,

Real chores, early mornings, doing the work of making things work.
It was the kind of work I complained about but, in truth, had been spared.

Taking out the garbage and washing windows did not count,
Not in comparison, not in this moment and not in the next few minutes

The dance took.
This did turn out to be my last high-school dance,

And the last for the group of us who would soon go out into the world.
Probably everybody has forgotten the dance.

Probably that girl I danced with has forgotten, but maybe not.
Maybe, like me, she felt something happen.

It wasn't love or something like that from the movies.
It was something bigger, more intimate, more honest.

It was the smallest electrical connection to difference—
We were, simply, different.

Not skin color, not visible things, but two hands
Speaking to each other, grasping each other and our worlds as well.

Perhaps it was a kind of love, after all.
Love, respect, wonder, sorrow.

It felt like the way static electricity can surprise you in its full
Half-second moment.

As with a small electric shock, there was nothing to romanticize,
Exactly, except to be dazzled by something bigger than you are,

Something you can't understand or explain.
In that roughness and in that moment, there was a tenderness

Beyond any real measure I had felt,
A moment in which something of the hard world

Kindly was revealed to me,
Something that had not been mine but was now.

My hand was soft, and hers was leather.
We were leading two different lives.

We lived on the border, and could talk about it easily.
But this was the border, too, the border I would carry with me

Every bit as much as the fence-now-wearing-the-glove-of-a-wall.
We danced, we laughed, and, I think, we both remember.

Mining Towns

We did not take from the mines—we gave to them:
Our short lives, our rough hands, our dark days.

For us, it was night when it was day,
The world turned around both outside and inside us.

Night was for sleeping, of course, but we could not—
Any kind of not-paying-attention was dangerous.

We knew this, had given fingers and arms to its teacher.
In this way, night itself became dangerous.

When we came out of the ground, we could only look around
Always watching for something, some out-of-place thing,

Knowing that it all depended on us, us personally,
Any way we turned, every time we moved.

Jugando Hoyos

We played a game called Hoyos, that name being what it was,
Holes—holes we dug easily in the dirt, into which, from a distance,

We tried to roll whatever we had that resembled a ball:
Marbles, a golf ball, a ping-pong ball, or a red rubber ball

Pulled from those old, wooden paddle toys
Where you bounced the ball tethered to a piece of elastic

Against the paddle as many times as you could.
We liked those red balls especially, and hated them too—

We left the staple on, maybe a little bit of elastic as well,
Which made the balls roll left and right in haunted ways,

A power we would later call science.
We put a small rock behind every hole the ball rolled into,

A way of tallying our efforts, a first, elemental arithmetic.
Our afternoons were made of these holes and the shouts we supplied,

Encouragements and jeers, the simple theater of the young.
We were masters, then, of the very small universe that was ours.

The game cost little, which was what we had.
It was a game that grew to be all games.

Hoyos. We call it soccer, now, or baseball, or football,
Clever disguises for what we feel inside when a ball is in motion.

We were kids then, inventing something for ourselves,
Something that moved in our lives when nothing else did,

Something that got us moving, something that moves us still—
Any game still a magnet to that moment, making our bodies twitch.

In Service to Service

Mosaics and jigsaws, however awkward we are,
Know that we are fractured and whole both.

We wear the cloak of invisibility,
Though it may not be the superpower we might once have imagined.

We are, because we serve, so often thought of as that service,
You and I constructed by what we do, not who we are.

There are no judges, only judgments. There are no food servers,
Only food, no electricians, only light. Fairly or unfairly,

Through hard days and whole years invisibly given, we measure ourselves.
No one sees the hours. No one lives them but us.

This is the great and good secret we carry: hard work.
At the end of a day, however, it is a graceful burden.

To serve is to worry so that worry does not become our greater legacy.
To serve is to find song so surprisingly

In the raising of bridges and the shortening of lines,
In the sharing of bread, and warmth, and laughter.

To be not tall, nor thin, not young,
But simply the giver of what might be given,

The hope-builder, the foundation-layer,
The lion of best things.

Let us act so that the universe might applaud this offering,
The exchange of who we are for what we become.

The great superpower we imagined invisibility to be—
Let us understand, we were right.

Taking Our Olympic Measure

Poetry was an Olympic event from 1912 to 1948.

Think of the records you have held:
For one second, you were the world's youngest person.

It was a long time ago, but still.
At this moment, you are living

In the farthest thousandth-of-a-second in the history of time.
You have beaten yesterday's record, again.

You were perhaps the only participant
But in the race to get from your bedroom to the bathroom,

You won.
You win so much, all the time in all things.

Your heart simply beats and beats and beats—
It does not lose, although perhaps one day.

Nevertheless, the list of firsts for you is endless—
Doing what you have not done before,

Tasting sake and mole, smelling bergamot, hearing
Less well than you used to—

Not all records are for the scrapbook, of course—
Sometimes you are the best at being the worst.

Some records are secret—you know which ones.
Some records you're not even aware of.

In general, however, at the end of a long day, you are—
Unlikely as it may seem—the record holder of note.

Judging Ourselves

Fairness is the one language
Best spoken loudly.

We are better today
Because of what has come before us.

We should thank ourselves,
That in some measure we have paid attention.

But now, we have traveled as far into the centuries
As human beings have ever gone.

We are today, at this moment, at the far edge of time.
Is this where we want to be? Are we the who

Our grandparents imagined we would be?
Is this the house we wanted to build?

Today and now, we are the builders. This is our house.
But it leaks. We know it is only partially built.

But we have the tools and history's blueprint.
In whatever way we pound the hammer—or the gavel—

We must build a life having imagined it well,
Able to move forward from having listened to one another,

Knowing we are at our best together. One CEO,
One goatherd, one copper miner is not enough.

We must speak reasonably to one another and, in turn,
We must listen for the best of what listening brings.

We must change where history has taught us
Change is needed, and be glad to do it.

We have the power to be rain in the desert for one another,
Living in a house whose roof is in good repair.

FIVE

Theirs is a short life of light and crawl

The Monsoon Wait

The monsoon has come again,
But every year it loses weight,

A little older, a little slower.
It's never as big as we remember it,

How it filled entire weekday afternoons.
Nevertheless, monsoon, this desert's old cousin,

Still has some life in it, some party,
Coming to visit, to stir things up.

We so sad, so hot in our clothes,
So wishful of other things and places—

We have so much beach here, it's true,
Though we also meant to ask for ocean.

We want everything, of course. We want perfect.
Monsoon, the crickets talk about you.

Rabbit and wren, coyote and creosote,
All of us make room for the little bit of you

We will get to spend time with. Monsoon,
We expect you to solve all our problems.

When you arrive, always in a cloud of dust—
So dramatic, you movie star—

We don't say so but we hope
You have brought presents for each of us.

We look at you with big eyes,
Heads down and sport caps in hand.

You laugh so hard you cry rain.
We laugh with you.

Old People of the Desert

The old people of the desert, their bristly gray hair
Turned to needles, their backs so often bent, their bodies thin—

They don't move very much anymore, except perhaps
To dance with the moods of the wind,

Their arms upstretched, their arthritic joints in evidence
Everywhere but without complaint. They sometimes wear

Mesquite green dresses, sometimes paloverde yellow.
Their songs seem quiet because each word takes a year to say.

They've stopped needing water very much.
They've stopped being in a hurry to get anywhere.

They still feel young but aren't—immobile as photographs,
These citizens of a next world, of this cactus-and-mesquite world.

Their great-grandchildren come to look at the plants in the desert
But do not see themselves—seeing instead branches, arms,

The many thousand hard fingertips and sewing needles out there,
The hard skins of the saguaro and barrel, the ironwood—

Not imagining that the creases in their own knuckles connect them
To those they were, these tree-and-cactus people, this place.

The visitors look at their knuckles and the creases in their hands
Not for a moment thinking they are looking into a mirror.

The Yearly Return of the Mockingbird, Who Reads His Story Aloud to the World

Early April and the mockingbird in the side yard wilds
In its many perfect sharp and eloquent songs,

So earnestly, so loudly, so confidently offered to the world
As if, because of them, Juliet would come winging in right then and there.

But the days go by and the songs are only more,
Movingly delivered so well that one might imagine the bird singing

In a tuxedo, on a stage, having prepared a lifetime for this moment,
But still no Juliet.

The habit of these birds is to return each year
To the place where they have had previous success in their amorous efforts.

But that is the point. This is not an unrequited song of invitation, after all—
One suspects many Amelias and Janets have answered the call.

But this bird remembers, waits for, longs for Juliet. That moment,
Even as, unfortunately, the days of April without her stretch on.

Woodpecker Knocking

The woodpecker knocks on the door relentlessly.
Come in, I say. But he does not.

Go away, I say, but he does not.
Of course, had he come in, what would we do,

A woodpecker in the house?
The invitation to come inside was disingenuous.

I should not have said *come in*, even in jest.
I didn't mean it. But a bird, who knows?

What else to be but trusting, if wary?
How else to get by in the fragile world

So full of humans and moths and caterpillars and bugs.
The knocking on the door, of course, that tapping:

The woodpecker was not knocking to come in.
It was announcing itself to another woodpecker,

A bird more to his liking than I would be,
A bird with which a full and loving life might be made.

Gray bird, huddled in the eaves, trying to hide.
Go away, he hopes, as quietly as he can. But I do not.

We are at a standstill. I shoo him off
Though from our history together I know he will be back.

A woodpecker does not give up. Through it all,
Somewhere, another woodpecker waits for the call.

The Migration of the Birds Away from Us

I see the noise but hear nothing.
My window is closed but my eyes are not—
And this is the way of things,
One sense becoming another in a heartbeat.

The workmen outside turn the caliche dirt
Slowly in the heat, slowly because they have to,
The way workers have done
These last ten and twenty thousand years.

Something comes of it—
The birds have been watching,
All this time, trying to add this business up
In the trill physics of thin song.

The birds do not run out of song,
The workers do not run out of earth,
Neither run out of time—
The world in this way is for them.

The birds, those gray songs themselves
On the wire, they have taken
Account, they have remembered
Us, even as we move on.

The memory of us is only noise now,
Sound curiously placed in the beak
Having traveled from the throat
Having traveled from the brain

Having traveled from the eye
Having traveled from the act.
Our memory, our echo, our time
Lives on the wind in their single notes.

That the birds have other songs,
That the songs have other sounds,
That the sounds have other stories
That are not us: We do not know it

But this is why the workmen turn the dirt.
This is why the workmen have to turn the dirt.
When the song of us is done, when we say
It is all too much—and don't we think it?

The birds, as they always have,
They will move on to other songs.
They will remember us at first,
But their children will forget the words.

One More Sonoran Summer

Here, when the first 100-degree day arrives,
Someone wins a contest, and they're happy.

Everyone else has lost, however, and knows
One hundred degrees is just the start.

One hundred ten feels much the same
When it comes, and it does—it most certainly does—

No lithe, impressive dodgeball move here—
One newspaper winner, again, but then the rest of us.

The humor wears thin, as do the constant complaints,
Finally, about how unbelievably, ridiculously hot it is.

So simply what follows, however, is our living.
The regular us, albeit slower, in hotter cars and sweating.

But us. Professors, miners, astronomers, librarians,
Candymakers. We go on in this place, this desert,

So full of apparently nothing—no skyscrapers out there,
Only cactuses, no freeways but arroyos. This desert,

So full of apparently nothing—but that trick is itself
The great mirage of the Sonoran Desert:

Along with the cholla and orange trees, the iguanas,
The thunderstorms, tortoises, turquoise, and tarantulas,

We are here, we have always been here, we will be here.
We stay inside, we move slowly, we go where we must.

We, too, are some of the animals of the desert, this whole world,
Baying at the moon and marveling at the jackrabbits' ears.

Desert Ocean

I have seen fish swim in the desert
As I threw them, these fish now fossils on rocks

My hands and arms sent flying.
I myself could not fly but these rock-fish could—

Swimming or flying, theirs was a life beyond my own
From a time, too, beyond my own.

Other things that could not fly flew anyway as well,
Dust motes, these plankton of the desert air in sunlight.

Other things that should not move moved anyway as well,
Semitrucks, pretend-animals, these great whales of the desert.

The ocean keeps its voice in the desert in more than fossil:
Saguaros with all their big arms are octopuses in disguise.

The sea turtle and the desert tortoise do not even try
To hide their family lineage. And birds, those fish of the air.

The mountains themselves suggest waves far in the past,
Fossilized now into this curious stateliness of memory,

A mountain being the photograph of a grandfather wave
Allowing us even to step onto the dirt of its old water.

As I stand, hands on hips, the shore here is of time, not place.
This desert, once and still ocean, waits for what life will come next.

Sonoran Sonnet

A small song, a small noise.
Sonora and *sonnet* come from the same etymological roots—

A desert and a poem sonorous, full of noise, clamor, sound and snap.
Words the narrating song of one, but the desert:

Words, sounds, its refrain—they are for the secret ears of the body.
Shall I compare thee to a summer's day?

Shakespeare, Petrarch, Rossetti—their sonnets may fill us with their haunt,
Browning, Donne, and all the rest. Good words and memorable.

But a summer day means something different in the Sonoran Desert,
Haunting just as much. The *¡ay Lázaro!* birds, the white-winged doves,

The mourning and Inca doves, their *calming-of-the-child* cooing in the quiet.
The cardinals, the cicadas, the yips and baying of coyote families,

The mustering of javelinas, the constant conversation of insects,
The small buzzing of a live world. The summer thunder.

I think of a hard rain first coming in the monsoon season, water
Drops hitting the dry mesquite pods making a wooden maraca sound, water

Hitting the million bone-dry pods from a long summer of never enough rain,
The seeds inside happy now, their small *ch-ch-ch* sound in the slightest wind.

Rain. Desert's first music. Cicadas will have been buzzing already.
The ocarina sounds of the doves make their sighing heard.

All the movement makes a small movement of air, enough to cool, words
Adequate in their wetness to make life just enough.

Poem and desert, a good marriage. Theirs is a short life of light and crawl,
Water, wind, words, music, and moment—so much to make life just enough.

The Water in All My Names

My family's names were like clouds—
They carried within them a lot of moisture.

This is a good thing since I live in the desert.
My names watered me and helped me to grow.

My last name is Ríos, which means *rivers.*
I got that name from my father.

My mother's last name was Fogg. Two *g*'s.
That's a lot of fog.

Her name is mine too—it's part of me.
All of us together, my family,

We were rare water in the desert,
Which still holds out its big saguaro arms for me.

Maybe I'm really a cactus too,
Or a coyote, or a mirage.

Maybe all that water made me
A sailor on the desert's invisible sea.

SIX

The world, the world

Boat in the Forest

In the forest there is the possibility of a boat,
The great timbers of a ship, strong branches

To hold up sails as if they were laundry,
To make a great perch in service to great birds,

To make an elegant jungle gym for those
Who would climb as if it were play.

A ship, after all, is many things.
And strong.

In the forest, a gold mine exists for the wanderer—
Tall wood to make the hull needed for a long journey.

In the desert there is not the possibility of a boat,
No great timbers for a ship, no strong branches.

In the desert there is, instead, the possibility of a dream,
A vast space in which to build a great idea,

A dream big enough and patient enough
To let a ship sail through it, however incongruously,

A ship fast and far and lucky enough
To find the Place at the End of Dreams,

That great starting point
Between water and earth,

That place waiting between the worlds we know.
Ocean or desert, forest or dream—

We will have used them all
On our way to the stars.

To Mars from Arizona

Saturday mornings were science fiction—
That is, on that day anything was possible.

We didn't have to go to the movies for that,
Though when we did, we were introduced to ourselves

More than anything. Ourselves in rockets,
Ourselves taking chances, ourselves speaking to the universe.

Outside the movies, we were still in them—
Our bikes were our rockets, our submarines, our jets.

But mostly, and first, our bikes were our horses
In this childhood West, a loyal, red Western Flyer

Taking me everywhere, up and down, fast and slow.
Only later did I understand it was my own legs

That did it all. My own legs and my arms to steer,
My own small, mighty lungs to shout—

A shout that would later become a song.
When they weren't horses, when my legs were tired,

When the shouts calmed down into just talking,
We bike-riders would sit, and find in that talking

The gold we had been looking for, though we didn't know it.
The gold was made of plans for Saturdays still to come—

Each of us had different ideas, but we all had them,
Speaking them confidently as if we were lions,

Deep-voiced and sure even in that quietude.
What would happen next was far away,

But even as we rested, something in us knew
We would catch the future no matter how fast it ran.

When They Land

When I put my socks on after getting up,
These small, perfect jackets for my feet,

Skin but not skin, close to skin,
These quiet caretakers, these wild

Happy letter L's, these sevens,
Not quite shoes, not quite not shoes,

I think of what will happen
When the first aliens finally land here.

We will look at them
But what we will see is their clothes.

Their suit pants. Their dress-up shirts.
The aliens will dress for us.

If they come here to Arizona,
They may be wearing formal shorts,

Sunglasses, carrying their water bottles—
Not guns, even if they look like guns

In whatever their hands will look like.
They will worry about what our hands hold.

They will wonder how we do what we do,
But they will drink water and breathe air too.

It's why they came here, specifically.
We are what they were looking for.

We are their aliens. They found us.
We are the star in a telescope a century ago.

We won't be able to communicate at first.
But we will compare socks.

The Sheet Music of Place

1

The river through its centuries has made a line on this place,
A child's line, wanting to be straight but distracted at every move,

A little left, a little fast, around a big rock, sliding straightaway
Through sand, this crawling, leaden line echoing

The line made by the tops of the mountains in silhouette against the sky.
The railroad track makes another line, a double line—

The highway too, and the telephone poles strung with wire.
All these lines work in sure if uneasy concert

Written on the arid air of this place, which has made everything
Dry and white, off-white, some darks but on their way to white,

All this landscape a great and delicate paper.

2

These lines make a musical staff borrowed from the world of dream,

The world that then fills these lines with its *profundo* notations,
The careful placement of one moving thing next to another,

The train engine and its cars, those drudging bass notes,
Birds everywhere in their trill, 64th notes every one,

Everything scored onto the pages of this world suddenly heard.
Day and night, that ceaseless baton, unforgiving metronome:

Bees lumber along but their work is to stop, whole stops and half,
Busy at their honeying, these respites of work, these moments loud

Too—resting the ear so as to hear composed this place into music—
Every sound a new performance of the great song of this world.

Today, Again

I walk because I have walked.
I hear because I have heard.

If this were the first time,
Walking would seem like a circus trick,

An invention, a curiosity, but useful.
Stop monkeying around,

My mother would have said—
You'll hurt yourself.

And I would have gone back to crawling,
Good boy that I was.

Growing up in the desert, there is a tired joke:
On rising, someone will invariably say,

Looks sunny today. It's never funny
But people say it anyway—fathers. You know the kind.

No one says, *I see you're walking today,*
Or, *I see you're breathing today.*

You just always are, always have, and it seems as if
You just always will.

What's Happening

There are times when nothing happens.
It belongs to no story, is recorded in no history book.

Nothing-happening happens when we leave the room.
It happens when we close the car door,

Leaving the car in the garage overnight. In truth,
It happens all the time, everywhere, all around the world.

But somewhere along the path, *something happening*
Got all the billing.

People started to go out of their way
To find something happening.

Nothing-happening got a bum rap.
Teenagers abandoned it, big towns avoided it,

Television shows and movies never talked about it.
Children sometimes bumped into it on summer vacations

But that was all. Nothing-happening couldn't give itself away, even to retirees.
Historians could shake their heads knowingly, asserting:

The Industrial Revolution about did it in.
Of course, the invention of neon lights didn't help.

All nothing-happening can do now is to clock in,
Another day at work, quietly rolling up its shopworn sleeves,

Putting on its soft leather apron: these
The quiet assurances of a thriving, healthy business.

Build the Word True

To make a word right, to say it true,
To spell it into existence,

To move from breath to being, thought to creature,
To build it part by part as if its letters were fixed timbers

Placed just so, a joist here, a two-by-four there,
All of it, every letter so critically important,

Even as more follows more. To understand
The chimney reach of a small *h*,

The dipping of a toe into the water of a *j*,
The free throw of a basketball in the lowercase *i*—

Drawing's the common language we speak,
Its wood and nails, its windows and floors.

It is a language made of what we do
No matter its name. With words, we cast spells:

These are the measures of the lives we lead,
The record of where we have been, and are now, and will go.

All languages seek to make a house. All words
Try to make a life at the kitchen table.

Let those words, those spells, be doorways.
Let their greater sentences be made of welcome mats.

Giving Ourselves

Some of us are given much—we have earned it,
We have won it, we have been given to.

Sometimes it is pure luck. The lottery,
Love, marriage, and that resulting job with a corner window.

Sometimes we lose
All of it, then find it again. Sometimes it is gone forever

And we must hope that someone does for us
What we did not do for them.

Through it all, through all the life we live
And lives we touch,

Ours is not just to give back—
Ours is to give back better than we were given.

Ours is to have made something, to have found
Ourselves finally at work, alive in the giving,

To have made a drink of water from all the oceans and the seas of the world.
To have made a poem from all the words in a dictionary.

The Suns and the Moons

We imagine one sun—though perhaps there are many,
The old one given up each evening to the west,

Spent, burnt, cooling, raging less, smaller, falling,
All to make way for a new one—clearly—each morning.

We imagine that we have only one moon as well,
Though we can plainly see how different it is each night.

Science assures us that these are momentary thoughts,
But we assume we have only one science as well.

I don't believe there is a new sun every day,
But I do save room for the possibility of a backup—

A stand-in, a stunt double. What about sick leave,
After all, or paternity leave, or jury duty. The dentist.

The moon doesn't have to dress up as much every night,
Having darkness to work with after all. A black dress

Hides much. A missed shower here or there, nobody notices.
It's a good job for the moon management team—

One night of all-out work every thirty days or so.
It's like baseball pitchers.

The world, the world—air, leaves, thunderstorms, desert,
Fruit. It is Eden enough, and mysterious still.

About the Author

Alberto Ríos, Arizona's inaugural poet laureate and a recent chancellor of the Academy of American Poets, is the author of thirteen books and chapbooks of poetry, including *The Theater of Night*, winner of the 2007 PEN/Beyond Margins Award; three collections of short stories; and a memoir about growing up on the border, *Capirotada*. His book *The Smallest Muscle in the Human Body* was a finalist for the National Book Award. Ríos is the recipient of numerous accolades, and his work is included in over 300 national and international literary anthologies. He is also the recent host of the PBS programs *Art in the 48*, for which he won a 2020 Rocky Mountain Emmy Award, and *Books & Co.* His work is regularly taught and translated and has been adapted to dance and both classical and popular music. Ríos is a University Professor of Letters, Regents' Professor, and the Katharine C. Turner Endowed Chair in English at Arizona State University. In 2017, he was named director of the Virginia G. Piper Center for Creative Writing. His other recent works are *Not Go Away Is My Name*, a book of poems, and *A Good Map of All Things*, a novel.

Poets for Poetry

Copper Canyon Press poets are at the center of all our efforts as a nonprofit publisher. Poets not only create the art that defines our books, but they read and teach the books we publish. Many are also generous donors who believe in financially supporting the larger poetry community of Copper Canyon Press. For decades, our poets have quietly donated their royalties, have directly engaged in our fundraising campaigns, and have made personal donations in support of the next generation. Their support has encouraged the innovative risk-taking that sustains and furthers the art form.

The donor-poets who have contributed to the Press since 2023 include:

Jonathan Aaron
Kelli Russell Agodon
Pamela Alexander
Joyce Harrington Bahle
Ellen Bass
Mark Bibbins
Sherwin Bitsui
Marianne Boruch
Laure-Anne Bosselaar
Cyrus Cassells
Peter Cole and Adina Hoffman
Elizabeth J. Coleman
John Freeman
Forrest Gander
Jenny George
Daniel Gerber
Julian Gewirtz
Jorie Graham
Robert and Carolyn Hedin
Bob Hicok
Ha Jin
Jaan Kaplinski
Laura Kasischke
Jennifer L. Knox
Ted Kooser
Deborah Landau
Sung-Il Lee
Ben Lerner
Dana Levin
Heather McHugh
Jane Miller
Lisa Olstein
Gregory Orr
Eric Pankey
Kevin Prufer
Paisley Rekdal
James Richardson
Alberto Ríos
David Romtvedt
Natalie Shapero
Arthur Sze
Elaine Terranova
Chase Twichell
Ocean Vuong
Connie Wanek-Dentinger
Emily Warn

Poetry is vital to language and living. Since 1972, Copper Canyon Press has published extraordinary poetry from around the world to engage the imaginations and intellects of readers, writers, booksellers, librarians, teachers, students, and donors.

WE ARE GRATEFUL FOR THE MAJOR SUPPORT PROVIDED BY:

academy of american poets

OFFICE OF ARTS & CULTURE
SEATTLE

ARTSFUND

THE PAUL G. ALLEN FAMILY FOUNDATION

Hawthornden Foundation

POETRY FOUNDATION

INGRAM CONTENT GROUP

the point
envision·enact·evolve

McSWEENEY'S

WASHINGTON STATE ARTS COMMISSION

ART WORKS.
National Endowment for the Arts
arts.gov

The Witter Bynner Foundation for Poetry

TO LEARN MORE ABOUT UNDERWRITING
COPPER CANYON PRESS TITLES,
PLEASE CALL 360-385-4925 EXT. 105

WE ARE GRATEFUL FOR THE MAJOR SUPPORT PROVIDED BY:

Anonymous
Jill Baker and Jeffrey Bishop
Anne and Geoffrey Barker
Donna Bellew
Lisha Bian
Will Blythe
John Branch
Diana Broze
John R. Cahill
Sarah J. Cavanaugh
Keith Cowan and Linda Walsh
Peter Currie
Geralyn White Dreyfous
The Evans Family
Mimi Gardner Gates
Gull Industries Inc.
  on behalf of William True
Carolyn and Robert Hedin
David and Jane Hibbard
Bruce S. Kahn
Phil Kovacevich and Eric Wechsler
Maureen Lee and Mark Busto
Ellie Mathews and Carl Youngmann
  as The North Press
Larry Mawby and Lois Bahle
Petunia Charitable Fund and
  adviser Elizabeth Hebert
Suzanne Rapp and Mark Hamilton
Adam and Lynn Rauch
Emily and Dan Raymond
Joseph C. Roberts
Cynthia Sears
Kim and Jeff Seely
Tree Swenson
Julia Sze
Barbara and Charles Wright
In honor of C.D. Wright
  from Forrest Gander
Caleb Young as C. Young Creative
The dedicated interns and faithful
  volunteers of Copper Canyon Press

The pressmark for Copper Canyon Press
suggests entrance, connection, and interaction
while holding at its center
an attentive, dynamic space for poetry.

This book is set in Janson.
Book design by Phil Kovacevich.
Printed on archival-quality paper.